The Lion's Roar

Two Discourses of the Buddha
from the Majjhima Nikāya

Translated from the Pali by
Bhikkhu Ñāṇamoli

Edited and revised by
Bhikkhu Bodhi

BUDDHIST PUBLICATION SOCIETY
KANDY   SRI LANKA

Published in 1993

Buddhist Publication Society
P.O. Box 61
54, Sangharaja Mawatha
Kandy, Sri Lanka

Copyright © 1993 Buddhist Publication Society

ISBN 955-24-0115-1

Typeset at the BPS
Text set in New Century Schoolbook

Printed in Sri Lanka by
Karunaratne & Sons Ltd.
Colombo 10

THE WHEEL PUBLICATION NO. 390/391

EDITOR'S NOTE

The original translations of the two suttas included in this booklet were made by Ven. Bhikkhu Ñāṇamoli. They are taken from his complete translation of the Majjhima Nikāya, which I have edited and revised for publication by Wisdom Publications, Boston (forthcoming, 1994/95). The numbers enclosed in square brackets are the page numbers of the Pali Text Society edition of the Pali text.

The introductions and notes are my own. In these the following abbreviations are employed:

DN	Dīgha Nikāya
MN	Majjhima Nikāya
Vbh.	Vibhaṅga
Comy.	Commentary

BHIKKHU BODHI

THE SHORTER DISCOURSE ON THE LION'S ROAR

Introduction

Among the hordes of animals that roam the wild, whether the jungle, the mountains or the plain, the lion is universally recognized to be their chief. The living embodiment of self-possessed power, he is the most regal in manner and deportment, the mightiest, the foremost with respect to speed, courage and dominion. The expression of the lion's supremacy is its roar—a roar which reduces to silence the cries, howls, bellows, shrieks, barks and growls of lesser creatures. When the lion steps forth from his den and sounds his roar, all the other animals stop and listen. On such an occasion none dares even to sound its own cry, let alone to come into the open and challenge the fearless, unsurpassable roar of the golden-maned king of beasts.

The Buddha's discourses, as found in the ancient Pali Canon, frequently draw their imagery from the rich and varied animal life of the luxuriant Indian jungle. It is thus not surprising that when the Buddha has occasion to refer to himself, he chooses to represent himself as the stately lion and to describe his proclamation of the Dhamma, bold and thunderous, as a veritable lion's roar in the spiritual domain. The Majjhima Nikāya, the Collection of Middle Length Discourses, contains two suttas which bear this metaphor in their title. These two—No. 11 and No. 12 in the collection—are called respectively the Shorter Discourse on the Lion's Roar and the Great Discourse on the Lion's Roar. The variation in their titles, signalled by the Pali words *cūḷa*, "minor," and *mahā*, "great," evidently refers at one level to their different lengths, the one being four pages in the Pali, the other sixteen. At another level, these different designations may allude to the relative weight of the subject matter with which they deal, the "great" discourse being a rare revelation by the Buddha of his exalted spiritual endowments and all-encompassing knowledge, which entitle him to "roar his lion's roar" in the assemblies of human beings and gods. Still, both suttas, as their controlling image suggests, are of paramount importance. Each delivers in its own way an eloquent and inspiring testimony to the uniquely emancipating nature of the Buddha's Teaching and the peerless stature of the Teacher among the spiritual guides of humanity.

* * *

The Pali Commentaries explain that there are two kinds of lion's roar: that of the Buddha himself and that of his disciples. The former is sounded when the Buddha extols his own attainments or proclaims the potency of the doctrine he has realized; the latter, when accomplished disciples testify to their own achievement of the final goal, the fruit of Arahantship. Viewed in the light of this distinction, the Shorter Discourse on the Lion's Roar exhibits a hybrid character, being a sutta spoken by the Buddha to instruct his disciples how they should affirm, in discussions with others who hold different convictions, the singular greatness of the Teaching.

§2. The Buddha opens the discourse by disclosing the content of this roar. He tells his monks that they can boldly declare that "only here" (*idh'eva*)—i.e. in the Dispensation of the Enlightened One—is it possible to find true recluses of the first, second, third and fourth degrees. The expression "recluse" (*samaṇa*) here refers elliptically to the four grades of noble disciples who have reached the stages of realization at which final deliverance from suffering is irrevocably assured: the stream-enterer, the once-returner, the non-returner and the Arahant. The "doctrines of others" (*parappavāda*), the Buddha says, are devoid of true recluses, of those who stand on these elevated planes. In order to understand this statement properly, it is important to distinguish exactly what the words imply and what they do not imply. The words do not mean that other religions are destitute of persons of saintly stature. Such religions may well engender individuals who have attained to a high degree of spiritual purity—beings of noble character, lofty virtue, deep contemplative experience, and rich endowment with love and compassion. These religions, however, would not be capable of giving rise to *ariyan* individuals, those equipped with the penetrative wisdom that can cut through the bonds that fetter living beings to saṁsāra, the round of repeated birth and death. For such wisdom can only be engendered on a basis of right view—the view of the three characteristics of all conditioned phenomena, of dependent arising, and of the Four Noble Truths—and that view is promulgated exclusively in the fold of the Buddha's Dispensation.

Admittedly, this claim poses an unmistakable challenge to eclectic and universalist approaches to understanding the diversity of humankind's religious beliefs, but it in no way implies a lack of tolerance or good will. During the time of the Buddha himself, in the Ganges Valley, there thrived a whole panoply of religious teachings, all of which proposed, with a dazzling diversity of doctrines and practices, to show seekers of truth the path to liberating knowledge and to spiritual perfection. In his frequent meetings with uncommitted inquirers and with convinced followers of other creeds, the Buddha displayed the most complete tolerance and gracious cordiality. But though he was always ready to allow each individual to form his or her own convictions without the least constraint or coercion, he clearly did not subscribe to the universalist thesis that all religions teach essentially the same message, nor did he allow that the attainment of final release from suffering, Nibbāna, was accessible to those who stood outside the fold of his own Dispensation. While this position may seem narrow and parochial to many today, when reaction against the presumptions of dogmatic religion has become so prevalent, it is not maintained by the Buddha as a hidebound dogma or from motives of self-exalting pride, but from a clear and accurate discernment of the precise conditions required for the attainment of deliverance.

The Buddha's statement on this issue emerges in at least two important passages in the Canon, each of which reveals, from a slightly different angle, exactly what those conditions are. One is found in the Mahāparinibbāna Sutta (DN 16/ii,151-52). While the Buddha was lying between the twin sal trees on the eve of his demise, a wandering ascetic named Subhadda came into his presence to resolve a doubt: he wished to know whether or not the other great religious teachers contemporary with the Buddha, who were regarded as saints by the multitude, had actually attained spiritual realization, as they claimed to have done. The Buddha shifted the burden of the discussion away from a question aimed at assessing particular individuals and rephrased it in terms of a general evaluative principle. He declared: "In whatsoever Dhamma and Discipline the Noble Eightfold Path is not found, there one cannot find true recluses of the four degrees of liberation. But in whatever Dhamma and Discipline the Noble Eightfold Path is found, there one can find the four types of true recluses." Then the Buddha imparted to Subhadda the information that was important for him to know: "In this Dhamma and Discipline the Noble Eightfold Path is found, and in it alone are found also the true recluses of the four degrees. Outside this Dispensation the four types of enlightened individuals are not to be found. The doctrines of others are devoid of true recluses." In this passage the thrust of the Buddha's explanation points to a particular method of practice as essential to the attainment of true realization. That method of practice is the training in the Noble Eightfold Path, and because this path, in its fullness and perfection, is unique to the Dispensation of a Fully Enlightened One, it follows that persons who have reached the planes of deliverance are unique to his Dispensation as well.

In the Shorter Discourse on the Lion's Roar the reason for the Buddha's exclusivistic claim does not focus upon practice but upon doctrine, upon the understanding of the nature of reality that separates his own Dhamma from all other attempts to comprehend the human situation. As the argument unfolds, the Buddha will show that the essential key to liberation, the key that he alone makes available, is the teaching of *anattā*, of non-self or egolessness, which is at the same time the boundary line that marks the difference between his own doctrine and the doctrines of other teachers.

§§3-4. After announcing the "lion's roar" in §2, in the next section the Buddha begins to construct an imaginary dialogue between "the wanderers of other sects," i.e. the proponents of the rival religious systems, and his own ordained disciples, the bhikkhus. In the first stage of the discussion, the wanderers ask the bhikkhus about the grounds on which they advance their seemingly sweeping claim. The Buddha advises the monks that they should answer by mentioning four reasons: that they have confidence in the Teacher, they have confidence in his Teaching, they have fulfilled the precepts of training, and their co-religionists, both monastic and lay, live together in cordial harmony. The wanderers, however, do not remain satisfied with this answer, but join issue with the bhikkhus by pointing out that the four reasons that the Buddhists have offered are also found in their own sects. Thus there seems to be no essential distinction between them that the bhikkhus can appeal to as the basis for their thesis.

§5. The Buddha does not meet this challenge with a direct reply, but instead approaches it via an indirect route. He enters upon this route by first clarifying, through questioning of the wanderers, the criteria of a truly emancipating teaching. As a matter of mutual consensus both the bhikkhus and the wanderers agree that such a teaching must posit a goal that can be attained only by those who have achieved complete purification: freedom from lust, hate and delusion, from craving and clinging, from arbitrary prejudices ("favouring and opposing"), and from the coils of "proliferation" (*papañca*), i.e. thought constructions born of craving and groundless speculation.

Although the bhikkhus and the wanderers both agree on these criteria, this does not suffice to establish that they are shared equally by the different spiritual systems, nor does this imply that they are capable of being fulfilled regardless of the specific doctrine to which one subscribes or the discipline in which one trains. To show, again in an indirect manner, that the outside systems are not capable of leading to final liberation, the Buddha points out that there are two broad "families" of views, diametrically opposed to each other, under which the wide diversity of speculative systems can be subsumed. These two views are called, in the sutta, the view of being (*bhavadiṭṭhi*) and the view of non-being (*vibhavadiṭṭhi*). The view of being is identical with eternalism (*sassatavāda*), the positing of some eternal entity or spiritual principle, i.e. a substantial self or soul, as the essence of the individual, and the positing of an eternal entity, such as a creator God or metaphysical Absolute, as the ground or source of the objective universe. The view of non-being is identical with annihilationism (*ucchedavāda*), the repudiation of any principle of continuity beyond death and the denial of an objective, transpersonal foundation for morality.

While those who adhere to the former view do concur with the Buddhists in accepting the efficacy of spiritual practice, their teachings, according to the Buddha, are not free of an erroneous grasp of actuality. They spring from a deep clinging to the notion of a permanent self, which issues in an edifice of doctrine designed to substantiate that idea and guarantee the immortality of the imagined self. Hence the Buddha traces this view to its root in the craving for being (*bhavataṇhā*), and he maintains that those who adopt such a view are for that very reason the victims, even though unwittingly, of craving and attachment. The view of non-being, on the other hand, arises from an attitude of contempt towards existence, and finds its root in the craving for non-being (*vibhavataṇhā*). The thinkers who adopt this view generally begin, as the Buddha does, by recognizing the pervasive nature of suffering; but instead of pursuing this suffering back to its true causes, they rush to an unwarranted extreme by declaring that the entire life-process comes to an absolute end with the breakup of the body at death, so that at death a being is annihilated and exists no more in any way.

Having isolated these two views and shown them in their mutual opposition, the Buddha then states that any "recluses or brahmins," i.e. spiritual teachers, who do not understand these views as they really are fail to measure up to the criteria of those who have achieved the final goal. They are still subject to lust, hatred and delusion, to craving and clinging, etc., and thus they cannot claim to be freed from the cycle of repeated birth and death. Only those who have comprehended these views, who see their dangers and have relinquished them, are accessible to the right view that leads beyond all erroneous extremes, and it is by the instrumentality of that view that they are capable of cutting off the defilements and arriving at release from the saṁsāric round.

§§9-15. Even at this point, however, the Buddha has not yet explicitly shown that liberation from cyclic existence is an exclusive prerogative of his own Dispensation. He has only left this conclusion as an inference for those who are already aware that his Dhamma makes known the middle way that transcends extremist views. In the present sequence, however, he will bring his argument to its conclusion by homing in on the crucial point that separates his own teaching from all other religious and philosophical systems. He takes up this task by way of an examination of the mental activity of clinging (*upādāna*). He states that there are four kinds of clinging: (1) clinging to sense pleasures; (2) clinging to speculative views regarding the self and the world; (3) clinging to rules and observances, i.e. to external rules, rituals and austerities in the belief that they lead to liberation; (4) and clinging to a doctrine of self, i.e. to a view of a truly existent self. The last type of clinging, the subtlest and most elusive of the group, is tantamount to what the texts refer to as "personality view" (*sakkāyadiṭṭhi*): the view of a substantial self taken to be either identical in some way to the five aggregates that constitute the personality, or to stand in some relationship to those aggregates (see MN 44/i,300, etc.).

The Buddha next points out that the recluses and brahmins who propose a path to liberation all declare that they propound "the full understanding of all kinds of clinging," a phrase the commentary to the sutta glosses as meaning the *overcoming* (*samatikkama*) of all kinds of clinging. However, the Buddha says, in spite of this claim, the other spiritual teachers recognize and attack only a limited number of the forms of clinging; at best, they might teach the overcoming of the first three forms of clinging. What they cannot teach, because they have not comprehended this for themselves, is the overcoming of clinging to a doctrine of self, and it is this fourth type of clinging that vitiates even the aspects of their teachings that are wholesome and praiseworthy. Because they perceive the dangers in the grosser types of clinging, they might urge their disciples to relinquish them, to give up sensuality, dogmatism and ritualism, and to cultivate in their place renunciation, detachment and equanimity. Thereby they can enjoin their disciples to engage in virtuous courses of spiritual practice, courses which have the potency to generate superior states of rebirth within the round of saṁsāra. However, what they have not discovered, because of the insurmountable limits to their range of understanding, is the buried root of the entire cycle of repeated existence, which consists precisely in that adherence to the notion of self. For this reason, the Buddha maintains, such a Dhamma and Discipline cannot show the way to the uprooting of the belief in self, and he therefore concludes that it is "unemancipating, unconducive to peace"—the final peace of Nibbāna. Being taught by one who is not a Fully Enlightened Buddha, such a system does not merit the confidence of those who can be satisfied with nothing less than complete release from all saṁsāric suffering.

In contrast to other spiritual teachers, the Buddha continues, he himself, the Tathāgata, describes the full understanding of all kinds of clinging, inclusive of the clinging to a doctrine of self. Recognizing the danger in views of self, aware that all such views, no matter how lofty, are undermined by a fundamental cognitive error, he proclaims a path that leads to the eradication of views of self in all their bewildering variety. Hence, the Buddha says, his Dhamma and Discipline is truly emancipating, truly capable of leading to final peace, promulgated by a Fully Enlightened One, the proper field of confidence for seekers of liberation.

§§16-17. In the final sections of the discourse, the Buddha will validate his claim regarding the emancipating quality of his Dispensation by showing how a disciple who undertakes the practice of his teaching can reach the fruit of final deliverance. He first takes up the four kinds of clinging, the subject around which the preceding portion of the exposition revolved, and connects this topic with another major principle of his doctrine, dependent arising (*paṭicca samuppāda*). By applying the principle of dependent arising, he traces clinging to its source in craving, and then, continuing this line of inquiry, he pursues the entire sequence of conditional factors at the base of saṁsāra back to its deepest and most pernicious root, ignorance (*avijjā*).

In the final paragraph he introduces a bhikkhu who arrives at the culmination of the path: one who develops wisdom to the fullest extent, abandons all ignorance, and arouses the liberating knowledge. Such a one no longer clings through any kind of clinging: he has eradicated all four types of clinging, including the clinging to a doctrine of self, and with their eradication has attained the final goal, the personal realization of Nibbāna right in this very life.

MAJJHIMA NIKĀYA NO. 11

The Shorter Discourse on the Lion's Roar
(*Cūḷasīhanāda Sutta*)

1. Thus have I heard. On one occasion the Blessed One was living at Sāvatthī in Jeta's Grove, Anāthapiṇḍika's Park. There he addressed the bhikkhus thus: "Bhikkhus."
– "Venerable sir," they replied. The Blessed One said this:

2. "Bhikkhus, only here is there a recluse, only here a second recluse, only here a third recluse, only here a fourth recluse. The doctrines of others are devoid [64] of recluses: that is how you should rightly roar your lion's roar.[1]

3. "It is possible, bhikkhus, that wanderers of other sects might ask: 'But on the strength of what (argument) or with the support of what (authority) do the venerable ones say thus?' Wanderers of other sects who ask thus may be answered in this way: 'Friends, four things have been declared to us by the Blessed One who knows and sees, accomplished and fully enlightened; on seeing these in ourselves we say thus: "Only here is there a recluse, only here a second recluse, only here a third recluse, only here a fourth recluse. The doctrines of others are devoid of recluses." What are the four? We have confidence in the Teacher, we have confidence in the Dhamma, we have fulfilled the precepts, and our companions in the Dhamma are dear and agreeable to us whether they are layfolk or those gone forth. These are the four things declared to us

by the Blessed One who knows and sees, accomplished and fully enlightened, on seeing which in ourselves we say as we do.'

4. "It is possible, bhikkhus, that wanderers of other sects might say thus: 'Friends, we too have confidence in the Teacher, that is, in our Teacher; we too have confidence in the Dhamma, that is, in our Dhamma; we too have fulfilled the precepts, that is, our precepts; our companions in the Dhamma are dear and agreeable to us too whether they are layfolk or those gone forth. What is the distinction here, friends, what is the variance, what is the difference between you and us?'

5. "Wanderers of other sects who ask thus may be answered in this way: 'How then, friends, is the goal one or many?' Answering rightly, the wanderers of other sects would answer thus: 'Friends, the goal is one, not many.'[2] – 'But, friends, is that goal for one affected by lust or free from lust?' Answering rightly, the wanderers of other sects would answer thus: 'Friends, that goal is for one free from lust, not for one affected by lust.' – 'But, friends, is that goal for one affected by hate or free from hate?' Answering rightly, they would answer: 'Friends, that goal is for one free from hate, not for one affected by hate.' – 'But, friends, is that goal for one affected by delusion or free from delusion?' Answering rightly, they would answer: 'Friends, that goal is for one free from delusion, not for one affected by delusion.' – 'But, friends, is that goal for one affected by craving or free from craving?' [65] Answering rightly, they would answer: 'Friends, that goal is for one free from craving, not for one affected by craving.' – 'But, friends, is that goal for one affected by clinging or free from clinging?' Answering rightly, they would answer: 'Friends, that goal is for one free from clinging, not for one affected by clinging.' – 'But, friends, is that goal

for one who has vision or for one without vision?' Answering rightly, they would answer: 'Friends, that goal is for one with vision, not for one without vision.' – 'But, friends, is that goal for one who favours and opposes, or for one who does not favour and oppose?' Answering rightly, they would answer: 'Friends, that goal is for one who does not favour and oppose, not for one who favours and opposes.'[3] – 'But, friends is that goal for one who delights in and enjoys proliferation, or for one who does not delight in and enjoy proliferation?' Answering rightly, they would answer: 'Friends, that goal is for one who does not delight in and enjoy proliferation, not for one who delights in and enjoys proliferation.'[4]

6. "Bhikkhus, there are these two views: the view of being and the view of non-being. Any recluses or brahmins who rely on the view of being, adopt the view of being, accept the view of being, are opposed to the view of non-being. Any recluses or brahmins who rely on the view of non-being, adopt the view of non-being, accept the view of non-being, are opposed to the view of being.[5]

7. "Any recluses or brahmins who do not understand as they actually are the origin, the disappearance, the gratification, the danger and the escape[6] in the case of these two views are affected by lust, affected by hate, affected by delusion, affected by craving, affected by clinging, without vision, given to favouring and opposing, and they delight in and enjoy proliferation. They are not freed from birth, ageing and death, from sorrow, lamentation, pain, grief and despair; they are not freed from suffering, I say.

8. "Any recluses or brahmins who understand as they actually are the origin, the disappearance, the gratification, the danger and the escape in the case of these two views are without lust, without hate, without delusion, without craving, without clinging, with vision, not given

to favouring and opposing, and they do not delight in and enjoy proliferation. They are freed from birth, ageing and death, from sorrow, lamentation, pain, grief and despair; they are freed from suffering, I say. [66]

9. "Bhikkhus, there are these four kinds of clinging. What four? Clinging to sensual pleasures, clinging to views, clinging to rules and observances, and clinging to a doctrine of self.

10. "Though certain recluses and brahmins claim to propound the full understanding of all kinds of clinging, they do not completely describe the full understanding of all kinds of clinging.[7] They describe the full understanding of clinging to sensual pleasures without describing the full understanding of clinging to views, clinging to rules and observances, and clinging to a doctrine of self. Why is that? Those good recluses and brahmins do not understand these three instances of clinging as they actually are. Therefore, though they claim to propound the full understanding of all kinds of clinging, they describe only the full understanding of clinging to sensual pleasures without describing the full understanding of clinging to views, clinging to rules and observances, and clinging to a doctrine of self.

11. "Though certain recluses and brahmins claim to propound the full understanding of all kinds of clinging ... they describe the full understanding of clinging to sensual pleasures and clinging to views without describing the full understanding of clinging to rules and observances and clinging to a doctrine of self. Why is that? They do not understand two instances ... therefore they describe only the full understanding of clinging to sensual pleasures and clinging to views without describing the full understanding of clinging to rules and observances and clinging to a doctrine of self.

12. "Though certain recluses and brahmins claim to propound the full understanding of all kinds of clinging ... they describe the full understanding of clinging to sensual pleasures, clinging to views, and clinging to rules and observances without describing the full understanding of clinging to a doctrine of self. They do not understand one instance ... therefore they describe only the full understanding of clinging to sensual pleasures, clinging to views, and clinging to rules and observances without describing the full understanding of clinging to a doctrine of self.[8]

13. "Bhikkhus, in such a Dhamma and Discipline as that it is plain that confidence in the Teacher is not rightly directed, that confidence in the Dhamma is not rightly directed, that fulfilment of the precepts is not rightly directed, and that the affection among companions in the Dhamma is not rightly directed. Why is that? Because that is how it is when the Dhamma and Discipline is [67] badly proclaimed and badly expounded, unemancipating, unconducive to peace, expounded by one who is not fully enlightened.

14. "Bhikkhus, when a Tathāgata, accomplished and fully enlightened, claims to propound the full understanding of all kinds of clinging, he completely describes the full understanding of all kinds of clinging: he describes the full understanding of clinging to sensual pleasures, clinging to views, clinging to rules and observances, and clinging to a doctrine of self.[9]

15. "Bhikkhus, in such a Dhamma and Discipline as that it is plain that confidence in the Teacher is rightly directed, that confidence in the Dhamma is rightly directed, that fulfilment of the precepts is rightly directed, and that the affection among companions in the Dhamma is rightly directed. Why is that? Because that is how it is

when the Dhamma and Discipline is well proclaimed and well expounded, emancipating, conducive to peace, expounded by one who is fully enlightened.

16. "Now these four kinds of clinging have what as their source, what as their origin, from what are they born and produced? These four kinds of clinging have craving as their source, craving as their origin, they are born and produced from craving.[10] Craving has what as its source ...? Craving has feeling as its source.... Feeling has what as its source ...? Feeling has contact as its source ... Contact has what as its source ...? Contact has the sixfold base as its source.... The sixfold base has what as its source ...? The sixfold base has mentality-materiality as its source.... Mentality-materiality has what as its source ...? Mentality-materiality has consciousness as its source.... Consciousness has what as its source ...? Consciousness has formations as its source.... Formations have what as their source ...? Formations have ignorance as their source, ignorance as their origin; they are born and produced from ignorance.

17. "Bhikkhus, when ignorance is abandoned and true knowledge has arisen in a bhikkhu, then with the fading away of ignorance and the arising of true knowledge he no longer clings to sensual pleasures, no longer clings to views, no longer clings to rules and observances, no longer clings to a doctrine of self.[11] When he does not cling, he is not agitated. When he is not agitated, he personally attains Nibbāna. He understands: 'Birth is destroyed, the holy life has been lived, what had to be done has been done, there is no more coming to any state of being.' "[12]
[68]

That is what the Blessed One said. The bhikkhus were satisfied and delighted in the Blessed One's words.

Notes

1. Comy. explains "lion's roar" (*sīhanāda*) as meaning a supreme roar (*seṭṭhanāda*), a fearless roar (*abhītanāda*), and a roar which cannot be confuted (*appaṭināda*). It adds: The roar about the existence of these four types of recluse only here is the supreme roar. The absence of any fear on account of others when one advances such a claim makes it a fearless roar. As none of the rival teachers can rise up and say, "These recluses also exist in our Dispensation," it is a roar which cannot be confuted.

2. Comy.: Even though the adherents of other sects all declare Arahantship—understood in a general sense as spiritual perfection—to be the goal, they point to other attainments as the goal in accordance with their views. Thus the brahmins declare the Brahma-world to be the goal, the great ascetics declare the gods of Streaming Radiance, the wanderers the gods of Refulgent Glory, and the Ājīvakas the non-percipient state, which they posit to be "infinite mind" (*anantamānasa*).

3. "Favouring and opposing" (*anurodha-paṭivirodha*): reacting with attraction through lust and with aversion through hatred.

4. Proliferation (*papañca*), according to Comy., generally means mental activity governed by craving, conceit and views, but here only craving and views are intended.

5. The adoption of one view entailing opposition to the other links up with the earlier statement that the goal is for one who does not favour and oppose.

6. Comy. mentions eight conditions which serve as the origin (*samudaya*) of these views: the five aggregates, ignorance, contact, perception, thought, unwise attention, bad friends, and the voice of another. Their disappearance (*atthaṅgama*) is the path of stream-entry, which eradicates all wrong views. Their gratification (*assāda*) may be understood as the satisfaction of psychological need to which the view caters, specifically the nurturing of craving for being by the eternalist view and of craving for non-being by the annihilationist view. Their danger (*ādīnava*) is the continued bondage they entail, by obstructing the acceptance of

right view, which leads to liberation. And the escape from them (*nissaraṇa*) is Nibbāna.

7. Comy. glosses full understanding (*pariññā*) here as overcoming (*samatikkama*), with reference to the commentarial notion of *pahānapariññā*, "full understanding as abandonment."

8. This passage clearly indicates that the critical differentiating factor of the Buddha's Dhamma is its "full understanding of clinging to a doctrine of self." This means, in effect, that the Buddha alone is able to show how to overcome all views of self by developing penetration into the truth of non-self (*anattā*).

9. Comy.: The Buddha teaches how clinging to sense pleasures is abandoned by the path of Arahantship, while the other three types of clinging are eliminated by the path of stream-entry. The path of stream-entry eliminates the other three clingings because these three are all forms of wrong view, and all wrong views are overcome at that stage. Although the statement that clinging to sense pleasures is abandoned by the path of Arahantship may sound strange, in view of the fact that sensual desire is already eliminated by the non-returner, the Ṭīkā (subcommentary) to the sutta explains that in the present context the word *kāma*, sense pleasure, should be understood to comprise all forms of greed, and the subtler types of greed are only eliminated with the attainment of Arahantship.

10. This passage is explained in order to show how clinging is to be abandoned. Clinging is traced back, via the chain of dependent arising, to its root-cause in ignorance, and then the destruction of ignorance is shown to be the means to eradicate clinging.

11. The Pali idiom, *n'eva kāmupādānaṁ upādiyati*, would have to be rendered literally as "he does not cling to the clinging to sense pleasures," which may obscure the sense more than it illuminates it. The word *upādāna* in Pali is the object of its own verb form, while "clinging" in English is not. The easiest solution is to translate directly in accordance with the sense rather than to try to reproduce the idiom in translation.

12. This is the stock canonical declaration of Arahantship.

THE GREAT DISCOURSE ON THE LION'S ROAR

Introduction

The Mahāsīhanāda Sutta, the Great Discourse on the Lion's Roar, is a text of awesome scope and power, one of those rare suttas in which the Buddha discloses the greatness and loftiness of his own spiritual endowments. Towards the end of the sutta, the Buddha says that he has reached his eightieth year, which allows us to place the discourse in the final year of his life. Thus the sutta serves as a convenient summation of the exalted qualities that enabled the Buddha to function so effectively as teacher and spiritual guide through the forty-five years of his mission.

It is not typical of the Buddha to extol himself, for he did not intend his Dispensation to evolve into a personality cult centred around himself as a charismatic and powerful leader. Throughout his ministry he constantly emphasized the primacy of his role as guide, as the discoverer and proclaimer of the path. His task is not to command reverence, but to steer his disciples onto and along the path, for it is only the practice of the path, the cultivation of the training, that can effect the deep interior purification by which one can reach the extinction of the defilements and liberation from suffering.

However, while the Buddha functions primarily as the revealer of the path, confidence in him as the Supreme

Teacher remains an essential element of the training. It is this confidence, freshly arisen, that induces the curious inquirer to cross the great divide that separates the admirer of the Dhamma from the practitioner, and it is this same confidence that drives the aspirant forward until the task of self-cultivation has been completed. Frequent reflection on the greatness of the Master inspires joy and courage, sustaining one's commitment during those dark periods when prospects for progress appear bleak, and desire and doubt—those twin conspirators—combine forces to attempt to persuade one of the futility of one's efforts. Hence, in order to provide a spur to awaken and nurture the confidence necessary to tread the path through its downward turns as well as its ascents, the Buddha on occasion offers us revelations of his "Buddha-*guṇas*," the excellent qualities of a Fully Enlightened One that entitle him to serve as the first of the Three Gems and Three Refuges.

One of the most impressive of these rare disclosures is the Great Discourse on the Lion's Roar. Spoken as a rebuttal to the charges of a renegade disciple who, in the midst of the populous city of Vesālī, had been denouncing the Buddha and attempting to dissuade others from following his teaching, the sutta recapitulates the various distinguished qualities of the Blessed One, with special emphasis upon his "ten Tathāgata powers" (*tathāgatabala*) and "four intrepidities" (*vesārajja*); the sutta also affords us a glimpse of the demanding ordeal he underwent over many past aeons seeking the path to deliverance. When it was first spoken, the sutta had such a powerful impact on one monk in the assembly that his bodily hairs stood on end, and thus, during an early period, the sutta was known by the alternative title "The Hair-raising Discourse." Even today, centuries later, the Great Discourse on the Lion's Roar can continue to serve as a fecund source of inspiration.

MAJJHIMA NIKĀYA NO. 12

The Great Discourse on the Lion's Roar
(Mahāsīhanāda Sutta)

1. Thus have I heard. On one occasion the Blessed One was living at Vesālī in the grove outside the city to the west.

2. Now on that occasion Sunakkhatta, son of the Licchavis, had recently left this Dhamma and Discipline.[1] He was making this statement before the Vesālī assembly: "The recluse Gotama does not have any superhuman states, any distinction in knowledge and vision worthy of the noble ones.[2] The recluse Gotama teaches a Dhamma (merely) hammered out by reasoning, following his own line of inquiry as it occurs to him, and when he teaches the Dhamma to anyone, it leads him when he practises it to the complete destruction of suffering."[3]

3. Then, when it was morning, the Venerable Sāriputta dressed, and taking his bowl and outer robe, went into Vesālī for alms. Then he heard Sunakkhatta, son of the Licchavis, making this statement before the Vesālī assembly. When he had wandered for alms in Vesālī and had returned from his almsround, after his meal he went to the Blessed One, and after paying homage to him, he sat down at one side and told the Blessed One what Sunakkhatta was saying.

4. (The Blessed One said:) "Sāriputta, the misguided man Sunakkhatta is angry, and his words are spoken out of

anger. Thinking to discredit the Tathāgata, he actually praises him; [69] for it is a praise of the Tathāgata to say of him: 'When he teaches the Dhamma to anyone, it leads him when he practises it to the complete destruction of suffering.'

5. "Sāriputta, this misguided man Sunakkhatta will never infer of me according to Dhamma: 'That Blessed One is accomplished, fully enlightened, perfect in true knowledge and conduct, sublime, knower of worlds, incomparable leader of persons to be tamed, teacher of gods and humans, enlightened, blessed.'[4]

6. "And he will never infer of me according to Dhamma: 'That Blessed One enjoys the various kinds of supernormal power: having been one, he becomes many; having been many, he becomes one; he appears and vanishes; he goes unhindered through a wall, through an enclosure, through a mountain, as though through space; he dives in and out of the earth as though it were water; he walks on water without sinking as though it were earth; seated cross-legged, he travels in space like a bird; with his hand he touches and strokes the moon and sun so powerful and mighty; he wields bodily mastery even as far as the Brahma-world.'

7. "And he will never infer of me according to Dhamma: 'With the divine ear element, which is purified and surpasses the human, that Blessed One hears both kinds of sounds, the heavenly and the human, those that are far as well as near.'

8. "And he will never infer of me according to Dhamma: 'That Blessed One encompasses with his own mind the minds of other beings, other persons. He understands a mind affected by lust as affected by lust and a mind unaffected by lust as unaffected by lust; he understands a mind affected by hate as affected by hate and a mind

unaffected by hate as unaffected by hate; he understands a mind affected by delusion as affected by delusion and a mind unaffected by delusion as unaffected by delusion; he understands a contracted mind as contracted and a distracted mind as distracted; he understands an exalted mind as exalted and an unexalted mind as unexalted; he understands a surpassed mind as surpassed and an unsurpassed mind as unsurpassed; he understands a concentrated mind as concentrated and an unconcentrated mind as unconcentrated; he understands a liberated mind as liberated and an unliberated mind as unliberated.'

(Ten Powers of a Tathāgata)

9. "Sāriputta, the Tathāgata has these ten Tathāgata's powers, possessing which he claims the herd-leader's place, roars his lion's roar in the assemblies, and sets rolling the Wheel of Brahmā.[5] What are the ten?

10. (1) "Here, the Tathāgata understands as it actually is the possible as possible and the impossible as impossible.[6] And that [70] is a Tathāgata's power that the Tathāgata has, by virtue of which he claims the herd-leader's place, roars his lion's roar in the assemblies, and sets rolling the Wheel of Brahmā.

11. (2) "Again, the Tathāgata understands as it actually is the results of actions undertaken, past, future and present, with possibilities and with causes. That too is a Tathāgata's power....[7]

12. (3) "Again, the Tathāgata understands as it actually is the ways leading to all destinations. That too is a Tathāgata's power.... [8]

13. (4) "Again, the Tathāgata understands as it actually is the world with its many and different elements. That too is a Tathāgata's power....[9]

14. (5) "Again, the Tathāgata understands as it actually is how beings have different inclinations. That too is a Tathāgata's power....[10]

15. (6) "Again, the Tathāgata understands as it actually is the disposition of the faculties of other beings, other persons. That too is a Tathāgata's power....[11]

16. (7) "Again, the Tathāgata understands as it actually is the defilement, the cleansing and the emergence in regard to the jhānas, liberations, concentrations and attainments. That too is a Tathāgata's power....[12]

17. (8) "Again, the Tathāgata recollects his manifold past lives, that is, one birth, two births, three births, four births, five births, ten births, twenty births, thirty births, forty births, fifty births, a hundred births, a thousand births, a hundred thousand births, many aeons of world-contraction, many aeons of world-expansion, many aeons of world-contraction and expansion: 'There I was so named, of such a clan, with such an appearance, such was my nutriment, such my experience of pleasure and pain, such my life-term; and passing away from there, I reappeared elsewhere; and there too I was so named, of such a clan, with such an appearance, such was my nutriment, such my experience of pleasure and pain, such my life-term; and passing away from there, I reappeared here.' Thus with their aspects and particulars he recollects his manifold past lives. That too is a Tathāgata's power....

18. (9) "Again, with the divine eye, which is purified and surpasses the human, the Tathāgata sees beings passing away and reappearing, inferior and superior, fair and ugly, fortunate and unfortunate, and he understands how beings pass on according to their actions thus: 'These worthy beings who were ill-conducted in body, speech and mind, revilers of noble ones, wrong in their views, giving effect to wrong view in their actions, on the dissolu-

tion of the body, [71] after death, have reappeared in a state of deprivation, in a bad destination, in perdition, even in hell; but these worthy beings who were well-conducted in body, speech and mind, not revilers of noble ones, right in their views, giving effect to right view in their actions, on the dissolution of the body, after death, have reappeared in a good destination, even in the heavenly world.' Thus with the divine eye, which is purified and surpasses the human, he sees beings passing away and reappearing, inferior and superior, fair and ugly, fortunate and unfortunate, and he understands how beings pass on according to their actions. That too is a Tathāgata's power....

19. (10) "Again, by realizing it for himself with direct knowledge, the Tathāgata here and now enters upon and abides in the deliverance of mind and deliverance by wisdom that are taintless with the destruction of the taints. That too is a Tathāgata's power that a Tathāgata has, by virtue of which he claims the herd-leader's place, roars his lion's roar in the assemblies, and sets rolling the Wheel of Brahmā.

20. "The Tathāgata has these ten Tathāgata's powers, possessing which he claims the herd-leader's place, roars his lion's roar in the assemblies, and sets rolling the Wheel of Brahmā.

21. "Sāriputta, when I know and see thus, should anyone say of me: 'The recluse Gotama does not have any superhuman states, any distinction in knowledge and vision worthy of the noble ones. The recluse Gotama teaches a Dhamma (merely) hammered out by reasoning, following his own line of inquiry as it occurs to him'— unless he abandons that assertion and that state of mind and relinquishes that view, then as (surely as if he had been) carried off and put there he will wind up in hell.[13]

Just as a bhikkhu possessed of virtue, concentration and wisdom would here and now enjoy final knowledge, so it will happen in this case, I say, that unless he abandons that assertion and that state of mind and relinquishes that view, then as (surely as if he had been) carried off and put there he will wind up in hell.

(Four Kinds of Intrepidity)

22. "Sāriputta, the Tathāgata has these four kinds of intrepidity, possessing which he claims the herd-leader's place, roars his lion's roar in the assemblies, and sets rolling the Wheel of Brahmā. What are the four?

23. "Here, I see no ground on which any recluse or brahmin or god or Māra or Brahmā or anyone at all in the world could, in accordance with the Dhamma, accuse me thus: 'While you claim full enlightenment, you are not fully enlightened in regard to certain things.' [72] And seeing no ground for that, I abide in safety, fearlessness and intrepidity.

24. "I see no ground on which any recluse ... or anyone at all could accuse me thus: 'While you claim to have destroyed the taints, these taints are undestroyed by you.' And seeing no ground for that, I abide in safety, fearlessness and intrepidity.

25. "I see no ground on which any recluse ... or anyone at all could accuse me thus: 'Those things called obstructions by you are not able to obstruct one who engages in them.' And seeing no ground for that, I abide in safety, fearlessness and intrepidity.

26. "I see no ground on which any recluse ... or anyone at all could accuse me thus: 'When you teach the Dhamma to someone, it does not lead him when he practises it to the complete destruction of suffering.' And seeing no ground

for that, I abide in safety, fearlessness and intrepidity.

27. "A Tathāgata has these four kinds of intrepidity, possessing which he claims the herd-leader's place, roars his lion's roar in the assemblies, and sets rolling the Wheel of Brahmā.[14]

28. "Sāriputta, when I know and see thus, should anyone say of me ... he will wind up in hell.

(The Eight Assemblies)

29. "Sāriputta, there are these eight assemblies. What are the eight? An assembly of nobles, an assembly of brahmins, an assembly of householders, an assembly of recluses, an assembly of gods of the heaven of the Four Great Kings, an assembly of gods of the heaven of the Thirty-three, an assembly of Māra's retinue, an assembly of Brahmās. Possessing these four kinds of intrepidity, the Tathāgata approaches and enters these eight assemblies.

30. "I recall having approached many hundred assemblies of nobles ... many hundred assemblies of brahmins ... many hundred assemblies of householders ... many hundred assemblies of recluses ... many hundred assemblies of gods of the heaven of the Four Great Kings ... many hundred assemblies of gods of the heaven of the Thirty-three ... many hundred assemblies of Māra's retinue ... many hundred assemblies of Brahmās. And formerly I had sat with them there and talked with them and held conversations with them, yet I see no ground for thinking that fear or timidity might come upon me there. And seeing no ground for that, I abide in safety, fearlessness and intrepidity. [73]

31. "Sāriputta, when I know and see thus, should anyone say of me ... he will wind up in hell.

(Four Kinds of Generation)

32. "Sāriputta, there are these four kinds of generation. What are the four? Egg-born generation, womb-born generation, moisture-born generation and spontaneous generation.

33. "What is egg-born generation? There are these beings born by breaking out of the shell of an egg; this is called egg-born generation. What is womb-born generation? There are these beings born by breaking out from the caul; this is called womb-born generation. What is moisture-born generation? There are these beings born in a rotten fish, in a rotten corpse, in rotten dough, in a cesspit, or in a sewer; this is called moisture-born generation. What is spontaneous generation? There are gods and denizens of hell and certain human beings and some beings in the lower worlds; this is called spontaneous generation. These are the four kinds of generation.

34. "Sāriputta, when I know and see thus, should anyone say of me ... he will wind up in hell.

(The Five Destinations and Nibbāna—In Brief)

35. "Sāriputta, there are these five destinations. What are the five? Hell, the animal realm, the realm of ghosts, human beings and gods.[15]

36. (1) "I understand hell, and the path and way leading to hell. And I also understand how one who has entered this path will, on the dissolution of the body, after death, reappear in a state of deprivation, in an unhappy destination, in perdition, in hell.

(2) "I understand the animal realm, and the path and way leading to the animal realm. And I also understand how one who has entered this path will, on the dissolution of the body, after death, reappear in the animal realm.

(3) "I understand the realm of ghosts, and the path and way leading to the realm of ghosts. And I also understand how one who has entered this path will, on the dissolution of the body, after death, reappear in the realm of ghosts.

(4) "I understand human beings, and the path and way leading to the human world. And I also understand how one who has entered this path will, on the dissolution of the body, after death, reappear among human beings.

(5) "I understand the gods, and the path and way leading to the world of the gods. And I also understand how one who has entered this path will, on the dissolution of the body, after death, reappear in a happy destination, in the heavenly world.

(6) "I understand Nibbāna, and the path and way leading to Nibbāna. [74] And I also understand how one who has entered this path will, by realizing it for himself with direct knowledge, here and now enter upon and abide in the deliverance of mind and deliverance by wisdom that are taintless with the destruction of the taints.

(The Five Destinations and Nibbāna—In Detail)

37. (1) "By encompassing mind with mind I understand a certain person thus: 'This person so behaves, so conducts himself, has taken such a path that on the dissolution of the body, after death, he will reappear in a state of deprivation, in an unhappy destination, in perdition, in hell.' And then later on, with the divine eye, which is purified and surpasses the human, I see that on the dissolution of the body, after death, he has reappeared in a state of deprivation, in an unhappy destination, in perdition, in hell, and is experiencing extremely painful, racking, piercing feelings. Suppose there were a charcoal pit

deeper than a man's height full of glowing coals without flame or smoke; and then a man scorched and exhausted by hot weather, weary, parched and thirsty, came by a path going in one way only and directed to that same charcoal pit. Then a man with good sight on seeing him would say: 'This person so behaves, so conducts himself, has taken such a path, that he will come to this same charcoal pit'; and then later on he sees that he has fallen into that charcoal pit and is experiencing extremely painful, racking, piercing feelings. So too, by encompassing mind with mind ... piercing feelings.

38. (2) "By encompassing mind with mind I understand a certain person thus: 'This person so behaves, so conducts himself, has taken such a path that on the dissolution of the body, after death, he will reappear in the animal realm.' And then later on, with the divine eye, which is purified and surpasses the human, I see that on the dissolution of the body, after death, he has reappeared in the animal realm and is experiencing painful, racking, piercing feelings. Suppose there were a cesspit deeper than a man's height full of filth; and then a man [75] scorched and exhausted by hot weather, weary, parched and thirsty, came by a path going in one way only and directed to that same cesspit. Then a man with good sight on seeing him would say: 'This person so behaves ... that he will come to this same cesspit'; and then later on he sees that he has fallen into that cesspit and is experiencing painful, racking, piercing feelings. So too, by encompassing mind with mind ... piercing feelings.

39. (3) "By encompassing mind with mind I understand a certain person thus: 'This person so behaves, so conducts himself, has taken such a path that on the dissolution of the body, after death, he will reappear in the realm of ghosts.' And then later on ... I see that ... he has reap-

peared in the realm of ghosts and is experiencing much painful feeling. Suppose there were a tree growing on uneven ground with scanty foliage casting a dappled shade; and then a man scorched and exhausted by hot weather, weary, parched and thirsty, came by a path going in one way only and directed to that same tree. Then a man with good sight on seeing him would say: 'This person so behaves ... that he will come to this same tree'; and then later on he sees that he is sitting or lying in the shade of that tree experiencing much painful feeling. So too, by encompassing mind with mind ... much painful feeling.

40. (4) "By encompassing mind with mind I understand a certain person thus: 'This person so behaves, so conducts himself, has taken such a path that on the dissolution of the body, after death, he will reappear among human beings.' And then later on ... I see that ... he has reappeared among human beings and is experiencing much pleasant feeling. Suppose there were a tree growing on even ground with thick foliage casting a deep shade; and then a man scorched and exhausted by hot weather, weary, parched and thirsty, came by a path going in one way only and directed to that same tree. Then a man with good sight on seeing him would say: 'This person so behaves ... that he will come to this same tree'; and then later on he sees that he is sitting or lying in the shade of that tree experiencing much pleasant feeling. So too, by encompassing mind with mind ... much pleasant feeling [76]

41. (5) "By encompassing mind with mind I understand a certain person thus: 'This person so behaves, so conducts himself, has taken such a path that on the dissolution of the body, after death, he will reappear in a happy destination, in the heavenly world.' And then later on ... I see that ... he has reappeared in a happy destination, in

the heavenly world and is experiencing extremely pleasant feelings. Suppose there were a mansion, and it had an upper chamber plastered within and without, shut off, secured by bars, with shuttered windows, and in it there was a couch spread with rugs, blankets and sheets, with a deerskin coverlet, with a canopy as well as crimson pillows for both (head and feet); and then a man scorched and exhausted by hot weather, weary, parched and thirsty, came by a path going in one way only and directed to that same mansion. Then a man with good sight on seeing him would say: 'This person so behaves ... that he will come to this same mansion'; and later on he sees that he is sitting or lying in that upper chamber in that mansion experiencing extremely pleasant feelings. So too, by encompassing mind with mind ... extremely pleasant feelings.

42. (6) "By encompassing mind with mind I understand a certain person thus: 'This person so behaves, so conducts himself, has taken such a path that by realizing it for himself with direct knowledge, he here and now will enter upon and abide in the deliverance of mind and deliverance by wisdom that are taintless with the destruction of the taints.' And then later on I see that by realizing it for himself with direct knowledge, he here and now enters upon and abides in the deliverance of mind and deliverance by wisdom that are taintless with the destruction of the taints, and is experiencing extremely pleasant feelings.[16] Suppose there were a pond with clean, agreeable, cool water, transparent, with smooth banks, delightful, and nearby a dense wood; and then a man scorched and exhausted by hot weather, weary, parched and thirsty, came by a path going in one way only and directed towards that same pond. Then a man with good sight on seeing him would say: 'This person so behaves ... that he will come to this same pond'; and then later on he sees

that he has plunged into the pond, bathed, drunk and relieved all his distress, fatigue and fever and has come out again and is sitting or lying in the wood [77] experiencing extremely pleasant feelings. So too, by encompassing mind with mind ... extremely pleasant feelings. These are the five destinations.

43. "Sāriputta, when I know and see thus, should anyone say of me: 'The recluse Gotama does not have any superhuman states, any distinction in knowledge and vision worthy of the noble ones. The recluse Gotama teaches a Dhamma (merely) hammered out by reasoning, following his own line of inquiry as it occurs to him'— unless he abandons that assertion and that state of mind and relinquishes that view, then as (surely as if he had been) carried off and put there he will wind up in hell. Just as a bhikkhu possessed of virtue, concentration and wisdom would here and now enjoy final knowledge, so it will happen in this case, I say, that unless he abandons that assertion and that state of mind and relinquishes that view, then as (surely as if he had been) carried off and put there he will wind up in hell.

(The Bodhisatta's Austerities)

44. "Sāriputta, I recall having lived a holy life possessing four factors. I have practised asceticism—the extreme of asceticism; I have practised coarseness—the extreme of coarseness; I have practised scrupulousness—the extreme of scrupulousness; I have practised seclusion—the extreme of seclusion.[17]

45. "Such was my asceticism, Sāriputta, that I went naked, rejecting conventions, licking my hands, not coming when asked, not stopping when asked; I did not accept food brought or food specially made or an invitation

to a meal; I received nothing from a pot, from a bowl, across a threshold, across a stick, across a pestle, from two eating together, from a pregnant woman, from a woman giving suck, from a woman lying with a man, from where food was advertised to be distributed, from where a dog was waiting, from where flies were buzzing; I accepted no fish or meat, I drank no liquor, wine or fermented brew. I kept to one house, to one morsel; I kept to two [78] houses, to two morsels; ... I kept to seven houses, to seven morsels. I lived on one saucerful a day, on two saucerfuls a day ... on seven saucerfuls a day; I took food once a day, once every two days ... once every seven days, and so on up to once every fortnight; I dwelt pursuing the practice of taking food at stated intervals. I was an eater of greens or millet or wild rice or hide-parings or moss or ricebran or rice-scum or sesamum flour or grass or cowdung. I lived on forest roots and fruits, I fed on fallen fruits. I clothed myself in hemp, in hemp-mixed cloth, in shrouds, in refuse rags, in tree bark, in antelope hide, in strips of antelope hide, in kusa-grass fabric, in bark fabric, in wood-shavings fabric, in head-hair wool, in animal wool, in owls' wings. I was one who pulled out hair and beard, pursuing the practice of pulling out hair and beard. I was one who stood continuously, rejecting seats. I was one who squatted continuously, devoted to maintaining the squatting position. I was one who used a mattress of spikes; I made a mattress of spikes my bed. I dwelt pursuing the practice of bathing in water three times daily including the evening. Thus in such a variety of ways I dwelt pursuing the practice of tormenting and mortifying the body. Such was my asceticism.

46. "Such was my coarseness, Sāriputta, that just as the bole of a tindukā tree, accumulating over the years, cakes and flakes off, so too, dust and dirt, accumulating

over the years, caked off my body and flaked off. It never occurred to me: 'Oh, let me rub this dust and dirt off with my hand, or let another rub this dust and dirt off with his hand'—it never occurred to me thus. Such was my coarseness.

47. "Such was my scrupulousness, Sāriputta, that I was always mindful in stepping forwards and stepping backwards. I was full of pity even for (the beings in) a drop of water thus: 'Let me not hurt the tiny creatures in the crevices of the ground.' Such was my scrupulousness.

48. "Such was my seclusion, Sāriputta, that [79] I would plunge into some forest and dwell there. And when I saw a cowherd or a shepherd or someone gathering grass or sticks, or a woodsman, I would flee from grove to grove, from thicket to thicket, from hollow to hollow, from hillock to hillock. Why was that? So that they should not see me or I see them. Just as a forest-bred deer, on seeing human beings, flees from grove to grove, from thicket to thicket, from hollow to hollow, from hillock to hillock, so too, when I saw a cowherd or a shepherd ... Such was my seclusion.

49. "I would go on all fours to the cow-pens when the cattle had gone out and the cowherd had left them, and I would feed on the dung of the young suckling calves. As long as my own excrement and urine lasted, I fed on my own excrement and urine. Such was my great distortion in feeding.

50. "I would plunge into some awe-inspiring grove and dwell there—a grove so awe-inspiring that normally it would make a man's hair stand up if he were not free from lust. When those cold wintry nights came during the 'eight-days interval of frost,' I would dwell by night in the open and by day in the grove.[18] In the last month of the hot season I would dwell by day in the open and by night

in the grove. And there came to me spontaneously this stanza never heard before:

> Chilled by night and scorched by day,
> Alone in awe-inspiring groves,
> Naked, no fire to sit beside,
> The sage yet pursues his quest.

51. "I would make my bed in a charnel ground with the bones of the dead for a pillow. And cowherd boys came up and spat on me, urinated on me, threw dirt at me, and poked sticks into my ears. Yet I do not recall that I ever aroused an evil mind (of hate) against them. Such was my abiding in equanimity. [80]

52. "Sāriputta, there are certain recluses and brahmins whose doctrine and view is this: 'Purification comes about through food.'[19] They say: 'Let us live on kola-fruits,' and they eat kola-fruits, they eat kola-fruit powder, they drink kola-fruit water, and they make many kinds of kola-fruit concoctions. Now I recall having eaten a single kola-fruit a day. Sāriputta, you may think that the kola-fruit was bigger at that time, yet you should not regard it so: the kola-fruit was then at most the same size as now. Through feeding on a single kola-fruit a day, my body reached a state of extreme emaciation. Because of eating so little my limbs became like the jointed segments of vine stems or bamboo stems. Because of eating so little my backside became like a camel's hoof. Because of eating so little the projections on my spine stood forth like corded beads. Because of eating so little my ribs jutted out as gaunt as the crazy rafters of an old roofless barn. Because of eating so little the gleam of my eyes sank far down in their sockets, looking like a gleam of water which has sunk far down in a deep well. Because of eating so little my scalp shrivelled and withered as a green bitter gourd shrivels

and withers in the wind and sun. Because of eating so little my belly skin adhered to my backbone; thus if I touched my belly skin I encountered my backbone, and if I touched my backbone I encountered my belly skin. Because of eating so little, if I tried to ease my body by rubbing my limbs with my hands, the hair, rotted at its roots, fell from my body as I rubbed.

53-55. "Sāriputta, there are certain recluses and brahmins whose doctrine and view is this: 'Purification comes about through food.' They say: 'Let us live on beans' ... 'Let us live on sesamum' ... 'Let us live on rice,' and they eat rice, they eat rice powder, [81] they drink rice water, and they make various kinds of rice concoctions. Now I recall having eaten a single rice grain a day. Sāriputta, you may think that the rice grain was bigger at that time, yet you should not regard it so: the rice grain was then at most the same size as now. Through feeding on a single rice grain a day, my body reached a state of extreme emaciation. Because of eating so little ... the hair, rotted at its roots, fell from my body as I rubbed.

56. "Yet, Sāriputta, by such conduct, by such practice, by such performance of austerities, I did not attain any superhuman states, any distinction in knowledge and vision worthy of the noble ones. Why was that? Because I did not attain that noble wisdom which when attained is noble and emancipating and leads the one who practises in accordance with it to the complete destruction of suffering.

57. "Sāriputta, there are certain recluses and brahmins whose doctrine and view is this: 'Purification comes about through the round of rebirths.' But it is impossible to find a realm in the round that I have not already [82] passed through in this long journey, except for the gods of the Pure Abodes; and had I passed through the round as a

god in the Pure Abodes, I would never have returned to this world.[20]

58. "There are certain recluses and brahmins whose doctrine and view is this: 'Purification comes about through (some particular kind of) rebirth.' But it is impossible to find a kind of rebirth that I have not been reborn in already in this long journey, except for the gods of the Pure Abodes....

59. "There are certain recluses and brahmins whose doctrine and view is this: 'Purification comes about through (some particular) abode.' But it is impossible to find a kind of abode that I have not already dwelt in ... except for the gods of the Pure Abodes....

60. "There are certain recluses and brahmins whose doctrine and view is this: 'Purification comes about through sacrifice.' But it is impossible to find a kind of sacrifice that has not already been offered up by me in this long journey, when I was either a head-anointed noble king or a well-to-do-brahmin.

61. "There are certain recluses and brahmins whose doctrine and view is this: 'Purification comes about through fire-worship.' But it is impossible to find a kind of fire that has not already been worshipped by me in this long journey, when I was either a head-anointed noble king or a well-to-do brahmin.

62. "Sāriputta, there are certain recluses and brahmins whose doctrine and view is this: 'As long as this good man is still young, a black-haired young man endowed with the blessing of youth, in the prime of life, so long is he perfect in his lucid wisdom. But when this good man is old, aged, burdened with years, advanced in life, and come to the last stage, being eighty, ninety or a hundred years old, then the lucidity of his wisdom is lost.' But it should not be regarded so. I am now old, aged, burdened with

years, advanced in life, and come to the last stage: my years have turned eighty. Now suppose that I had four disciples with a hundred years' lifespan, perfect in mindfulness, retentiveness, memory and lucidity of wisdom.[21] Just as a skilled archer, trained, practised and tested, could easily shoot a light arrow across the shadow of a palm tree, suppose that they were even to that extent perfect in mindfulness, retentiveness, [83] memory and lucidity of wisdom. Suppose that they continuously asked me about the four foundations of mindfulness and that I answered them when asked and that they remembered each answer of mine and never asked a subsidiary question or paused except to eat, drink, consume food, taste, urinate, defecate and rest in order to remove sleepiness and tiredness. Still the Tathāgata's exposition of the Dhamma, his explanations of factors of the Dhamma, and his replies to questions would not yet come to an end, but meanwhile those four disciples of mine with their hundred years' lifespan would have died at the end of those hundred years. Sāriputta, even if you have to carry me about on a bed, still there will be no change in the lucidity of the Tathāgata's wisdom.

63. "Rightly speaking, were it to be said of anyone: 'A being not subject to delusion has appeared in the world for the welfare and happiness of many, out of compassion for the world, for the good, welfare and happiness of gods and humans,' it is of me indeed that rightly speaking this should be said."

64. Now on that occasion the Venerable Nāgasamāla was standing behind the Blessed One fanning him.[22] Then he said to the Blessed One: "It is wonderful, venerable sir, it is marvellous! As I listened to this discourse on the Dhamma, the hairs of my body stood up. Venerable sir, what is the name of this discourse on the Dhamma?"

"As to that, Nāgasamāla, you may remember this discourse on the Dhamma as 'The Hair-raising Discourse.' "[23]

That is what the Blessed One said. The Venerable Nāgasamāla was satisfied and delighted in the Blessed One's words.

Notes

1. The story of Sunakkhatta's defection is found in the Pāṭika Sutta (DN 24). He became dissatisfied with the Buddha and left the Order because the Buddha would not perform miracles for him or explain to him the beginning of things. He also showed great admiration for those who engaged in self-mortification, and probably resented the Buddha for emphasizing a "middle way" that condemned such extreme austerities as unprofitable.

2. Superhuman states (*uttari manussadhammā*) are states, virtues or attainments higher than the ordinary human virtues comprised in the ten wholesome courses of action; they include the jhānas, direct knowledges (*abhiññā*), the paths and the fruits. "Distinction in knowledge and vision worthy of the noble ones" (*alamariyañāṇadassanavisesa*), an expression frequently occurring in the suttas, signifies all higher degrees of meditative knowledge characteristic of the noble individual. In the present context, according to Comy., it means specifically the supramundane path, which Sunakkhatta is thus denying of the Buddha.

3. The thrust of his criticism is that the Buddha teaches a doctrine that he has merely worked out in thought rather than one he has realized through transcendental wisdom. Apparently, Sunakkhatta believes that being led to the complete destruction of suffering is, as a goal, inferior to the acquisition of miraculous powers.

4. All the sections to follow are intended as a rebuttal of Sunakkhatta's charge against the Buddha. §§6-8 cover the first three of the six direct knowledges, the last three appearing as

the last of the ten powers of the Tathāgata. The latter, according to Comy., are to be understood as powers of knowledge (*ñāṇabala*) that are acquired by all Buddhas as the outcome of their accumulations of merit. The Vibhaṅga of the Abhidhamma Piṭaka provides an elaborate analysis of them, the gist of which will be discussed in subsequent notes.

5. Comy.: The Wheel of Brahmā (*brahmacakka*) is the supreme, best, most excellent wheel, the Wheel of the Dhamma (*dhammacakka*). This has two aspects: the knowledge of penetration (*paṭivedhañāṇa*) and the knowledge of teaching (*desanāñāṇa*). The knowledge of penetration, by which the Buddha penetrates the truth of the Dhamma, is produced from wisdom and leads to the attainment of the noble fruit for himself; the knowledge of teaching, by which the Buddha is qualified to expound the Dhamma perfectly to others, is produced from compassion and leads others to the attainment of the noble fruit.

6. Comy. glosses *ṭhāna* as cause or ground (*kāraṇa*) and explains: "Such and such dhammas are causes (*hetu*), conditions (*paccaya*), for the arising of such and such dhammas: that is *ṭhāna*. Such and such dhammas are not causes, not conditions, for the arising of such and such dhammas: that is *aṭṭhāna*. Knowing that, he understands *ṭhāna* as *ṭhāna* and *aṭṭhāna* as *aṭṭhāna* (i.e. causal occasion as causal occasion, and non-causal occasion as non-causal occasion)." Comy. also refers to the different explanation in the Vibhaṅga, apparently regarding both explanations as acceptable.

Vbh. §809 explains this knowledge with reference to MN 115 as the Buddha's knowledge of what is possible and what is impossible, e.g. it is impossible that a person possessed of right view should regard any formations as permanent or as pleasurable, or anything whatever as self, while it is possible that a worldling will regard things in such an erroneous way. It is impossible for a person possessed of right view to commit the five heinous crimes (matricide, parricide, the murder of an Arahant, the wounding of a Buddha, causing a schism in the Sangha), while it is possible for a worldling to commit such crimes, etc. etc.

7. Vbh. §810: "Herein, the Tathāgata comprehends that there are some evil actions performed which do not mature because they are prevented from maturing by a fortunate rebirth, a fortunate body, a fortunate time, a fortunate effort, while there are some evil actions performed which mature because of an unfortunate rebirth, etc. There are some good actions which do not mature because of an unfortunate rebirth, etc., while there are some good actions which mature because of a fortunate rebirth, etc." (condensed).

8. Vbh. §811: "Herein, the Tathāgata comprehends thus: 'This is the path, this is the practice leading to hell, to the animal realm, to the plane of ghosts, to the human realm, to the realm of the gods, to deliverance.'" This knowledge will be elaborated upon below in §§35-42.

9. Vbh. §812: "The Tathāgata comprehends the different aggregates, the different sense bases, the different elements; he comprehends the different worlds that have many elements, different elements."

10. Vbh. §813: "The Tathāgata understands that beings are of inferior inclinations and superior inclinations, and that they gravitate towards those who share their own inclinations" (condensed).

11. Vbh. §§814-27 gives a detailed analysis. Comy. states the meaning more concisely as the Tathāgata's knowledge of the superiority and inferiority of beings' faculties of faith, energy, mindfulness, concentration and wisdom.

12. Vbh. §828: "The defilement (*sankilesa*) is a state partaking of deterioration; cleansing (*vodāna*) is a state partaking of distinction; emergence (*vuṭṭhāna*) is both cleansing and the rising out of an attainment. The eight liberations (*vimokkha*) are enumerated, e.g. at DN 15/ii,70-71, and comprise three liberations pertaining to the realm of material form, the four immaterial attainments, and the cessation of perception and feeling. The nine attainments (*samāpatti*) are the four jhānas, the four immaterial attainments, and cessation.

13. The idiom *yathābhataṁ nikkhitto evaṁ niraye* is knotty;

the rendering here follows the gloss of Comy.: "He will be put in hell as if carried off and put there by the wardens of hell." Although such a fate may sound excessively severe merely for verbal denigration, it should be remembered that he is maligning a Fully Enlightened Buddha with a mind of hatred, and his intention in so doing is to discourage others from entering upon the path that could lead them to complete liberation from suffering.

14. The four kinds of intrepidity (*vesārajja*: also rendered "grounds of self-confidence") may be divided into two pairs. The first pair relates mainly to the internal qualities of the Buddha, his achievement of personal perfection, while the second pair has an outward orientation, being concerned primarily with his qualifications as a teacher. The first intrepidity confirms his attainment of supreme enlightenment and the removal of all obscuration regarding the range of what may be known; it points to the Buddha's acquisition of omniscience (*sabbaññutañāṇa*). The second underlines his complete purity through the destruction of all defilements; it points to his achievement of the fruit of Arahantship. The third means that the Buddha's understanding of obstructions to the goal is unimpeachable, while the fourth confirms the efficacy of the Dhamma in accomplishing its intended purpose, namely, leading the practitioner to complete release from suffering.

15. In later Buddhist tradition the *asuras*, titans or "anti-gods," are added as a separate realm to make the "six destinations" familiar from the Tibetan Wheel of Life.

16. Comy.: Even though the description is the same as that of the bliss of the heavenly world, the meaning is different. For the bliss of the heavenly world is not really extremely pleasant because the fevers of lust, etc. are still present there. But the bliss of Nibbāna is extremely pleasant in every way through the subsiding of all fevers.

17. Comy. explains that at this juncture the Buddha related this account of his past ascetic practices because Sunakkhatta was a great admirer of extreme asceticism (as is clear from the Pāṭika Sutta) and the Buddha wanted to make it known that there was no one who could equal him in the practice of austeri-

ties. §§44-56 apparently deal with the Bodhisatta's striving during the six years' period of austerities in his last existence, while §§57-61 refer back to his previous existences as a seeker of enlightenment.

18. The "eight-days' interval of frost" is a regular cold spell which occurs in South Asia in late December or early January.

19. That is, they hold the view that beings are purified by reducing their intake of food.

20. Rebirth into the Pure Abodes (*suddhāvāsa*) is possible only for non-returners.

21. The Pali for the four terms is: *sati, gati, dhiti, paññāveyyattiya*. Comy. explains *sati* as the ability to grasp in mind a hundred or a thousand phrases as they are being spoken; *gati*, the ability to bind them and retain them in the mind; *dhiti*, the ability to recite back what has been grasped and retained; and *paññāveyyattiya*, the ability to discern the meaning and logic of those phrases.

22. The Venerable Nāgasamāla had been a personal attendant of the Buddha during the first twenty years of his ministry.

23. *Lomahaṁsanapariyāya*. The sutta is referred to by that name at *Milindapañha*, p. 398, and in the commentary to the Digha Nikāya.